WORLD'S GREATEST ATHLETES

Mat HOFFMAN

By Bob Woods

The Child's World
www.childsworld.com

Published in the United States of America by The Child's World®
P.O. Box 326 • Chanhassen, MN 55317-0326
800-599-READ • www.childsworld.com

ACKNOWLEDGMENTS

The Child's World®: Mary Berendes, Publishing Director

Produced by Shoreline Publishing Group LLC
President / Editorial Director: James Buckley, Jr.
Designer: Tom Carling, carlingdesign.com
Assistant Editor: Ellen Labrecque

Photo Credits
Cover: Getty Images.
Interior: All photos by Getty Images except for the following:
Icon Images: 3, 9, 19; WireImage: 5.

LIBRARY OF CONGRESS
CATALOGING-IN-PUBLICATION DATA

Woods, Bob.
  Mat Hoffman / by Bob Woods.
      p. cm. — (The world's greatest athletes)
  Includes bibliographical references and index.
  ISBN 1-59296-755-8 (library bound : alk. paper)
  1. Hoffman, Mat, 1972—Juvenile literature. 2. Cyclists—United
States—Biography—Juvenile literature. 3. Bicycle motocross—
Juvenile literature. I. Title. II. Series.
  GV1051.H64W66 2006
  796.6'2092—dc22
                                                    2006006287

4074

CONTENTS

Greatest Show on Two Wheels

YOU CAN'T TALK ABOUT FREESTYLE BMX AND stunt bike riding without including MAT.

Although he's now 34, and his body can't take the bump and grind of competition anymore, Mat Hoffman—"the Condor"—remains a BMX fan favorite. He burst onto the scene in 1985 as a super-talented 13-year-old **amateur**. At 17, he became the youngest-ever professional BMX freestyle rider.

Mat revolutionized freestyle BMX, inventing more than 100 different tricks and jumps. He nailed the sport's first "900"—two-and-a-half complete **revolutions** in midair— in 1989. He won 10 BMX World Championships and two X Games gold medals. He retired from competition in 2002, but only after wowing the X Games fans with a no-handed 900!

As high as he flies though, the Condor has crashed plenty of times. He has broken 50 bones, suffered many **concussions**, and had 17 operations.

When he's not riding (and crashing), he's a businessman, too. He is the founder and owner of several companies, and video games featuring him are big sellers. The sport of freestyle BMX boomed in large part because of Mat Hoffman.

Rider and businessman Mat Hoffman is by far the most important person in BMX freestyle, on and off the ramp.

CHAPTER 1

Look! Up in the Sky—It's Mat!

MATHEW T HOFFMAN WAS BORN ON JANUARY 9, 1972, in Edmond, Oklahoma. He was the fourth child of Matthew and Joni Hoffman. His parents dropped one "t" from Dad's name to get Mathew, and then recycled that single letter for his middle name.

Mat could have easily been named Daredevil. He broke his first bone at age 6—his left leg while chasing a Frisbee. He broke his wrist two days later when he fell off a 15-foot slide. By then, Mat was already doing back flips on the family trampoline. Before long, he was doing stunts on his bicycle as well. He fondly recalls jumping his bike off the roof of the house and landing in the swimming pool.

Mat was 11 when he got his first true BMX bike, a red Mongoose with 20-inch wheels. He quickly

Mat's total fearlessness in doing aerial stunts like this one have made him a world champion—and world famous.

BMX bikes were first only used in races on short, hilly dirt tracks. Riders found that jumps let them do tricks, too.

decided that bicycle motocross racing wasn't for him. Instead he liked catching air off the jumps along the course. The sport of freestyle BMX fit Mat's wild personality.

"It was art instead of competition," he told Britain's *Observer Sport Monthly* in 2002, comparing freestyle riding to other team sports. "There were so many ways to express yourself. Your personality made the rules, and you didn't need a coach to tell you what was possible."

Mat's first experience on a vertical ramp was scary and eye opening. He took his bike to the top of a homemade quarterpipe. His brother Todd held onto the back of the bike and promised not to let go. Of course, Todd did let go and Mat went flying down the side of the pipe. Instead of being upset, Mat wanted to try it again . . . and again . . . and again.

Mat's life soon revolved around BMX freestyling. He and some friends formed a team

Mat is soaring off a halfpipe here, but he started on a wooden backyard quarterpipe about half this size.

and performed at local events. Mat always stood out though, going for higher air and creating new versions of stunts. At 13, he became a top amateur competitor, first on the local scene around Oklahoma City, and soon after on the national stage.

Young Mat

Growing up in Edmond, Oklahoma, Mat developed his lifelong love of flying quite early. He and his older brothers, Todd and Travis, built wooden airplanes. "I would sit in these splintery things for hours, pretending we were airborne," Mat writes in his autobiography, *The Ride of My Life*.

He also attempted liftoff in a homemade hang glider from a swing-set slide, but crashed. And after seeing a movie on TV, he tried jumping off the roof of the family barn onto a horse. "The horse moved as I jumped," he recalls, "and I landed on the ground, heels first. I had bruised feet for weeks."

Mat had no better luck after watching an old television show called "The Flying Nun." He tried to leap off his roof while holding an umbrella. "That didn't work either," he confesses.

The sky was the limit for young Mat, who was able to turn his love for action into a successful BMX career.

After winning a contest in New York, 15-year-old Mat was asked to join a BMX team, sponsored by the makers of Skyway bikes. The team toured the country and put on shows.

In 1988, Mat switched to the freestyle team sponsored by Haro. Its founder, Bob Haro, is recognized as one of the pioneers of BMX. Mat was only 16 when he started touring with the biggest names in the booming action sport, such as Ron Wilkerson, Dave Nourie, Joe Johnson, and Dennis McCoy. In no time, Mat had outflown them all and was among the world's **elite** BMX freestylers.

Freestyle BMX demands the body control of a gymnast. Mat is high above the ramp when he pulls his feet off the bike here.

CHAPTER 2

Turning Pro— Turning Heads

SHORTLY AFTER HIS 17TH BIRTHDAY IN 1989, MAT celebrated by joining the professional ranks—in spectacular style. Mat won a King of Vert (KOV) competition in California, his first title as a pro.

"I unleashed everything I had," he writes in his autobiography, "I busted out with a new trick I'd just invented. I blasted about five feet out of the halfpipe, removed all my limbs from bike contact, then grabbed back in time to re-enter the ramp backward. I called it a nothing fakie."

Also in 1989, Mat added a thumb to his growing list of broken bones. His thumb was broken before he arrived in Waterloo, Ontario, for a KOV competition. Cast and all, he still tried the "900." Only a handful of top contenders had ever tried the trick—two and a half airborne revolutions off the vert ramp. No one had ever nailed it. Mat landed the trick and sent the stadium full of fans into a frenzy.

"When I landed it, the feeling was amazing," he told EXPN.com in 2001. "Anytime you push yourself through **uncharted** territory, it is the best, most satisfying feeling."

Mat didn't wait long after his fantastic 900 feat to make more BMX history. Another trick that no vert rider had landed was a back flip. Even the daredevilish Mat knew a crash on this one could break his neck. He practiced by doing flips, first off a lakeside dock into the water, and then onto a pile of old mattresses. His ultimate goal was a back flip fakie off a quarterpipe, where he'd land on the ramp backwards.

In 1990, Mat decided to try the trick at a BMX competition in Paris, France. He hit the quarterpipe at full speed, zoomed to the top, went airborne, and leaned back as far as he could. He wanted to be safely away from the ramp as he went up and over. "I remember being upside down," Mat recalls in The Ride of My Life, "seeing flashbulbs popping. I don't think the French spectators were ready for what

Here's an upside-down Mat from 2002, continuing the tradition of mind-blowing tricks he started in 1990 (inset).

they saw, but the reaction was thunderous." The bike magazine *Go* ran a photo of Mat's trick on its July 1990 cover, calling it the "Sickest Trick Ever."

There was a sicker trick to come that year from the 18-year-old—but not before a family tragedy struck. His mom died from cancer during

In His Own Words

Mat Hoffman has broken nearly every bone in his body. And that's despite safety equipment.

"When I got into bike riding, I was the only kid who had a full-face helmet and wore a chest protector," Mat told Scholastic Choices *in 2005. "People were like, 'Who's this kid?' But then they realized that you only get two arms and two legs, and you've got to protect them. It started catching on and influenced other kids to respect the dangers of the sport and to wear the proper gear."*

Here are recommended pieces of safety gear for BMX freestylers:

- Full-face helmet

- Knee pads, elbow pads

- Chest protector

- Padded gloves with good grips

- Shoes with soft soles that will stick to pedals

- Pads on the bike's top tube, the handlebar's crossbar

Mat gets some nice air above the rim of the halfpipe, giving the riders waiting their turn a perfect view of The Condor.

the summer of 1990. With a heavy heart, Mat flew to England to perform in a demonstration. There, he met a young fan there who was dying from cancer. Thinking it would give the boy a boost, Mat attempted a never-been-done-before flair: a back flip with a 180-degree twist.

Mat crashed on his first try, but picked himself up and attempted another. "His second try, he stuck it," remembers Kevin Martin, the announcer that day. "Everyone there was totally blown away. I still get goose bumps thinking about that one trick."

CHAPTER 3

Putting His Skills to Work

BY THE EARLY 1990S, MAT AND HIS FELLOW BMX freestyle riders were dazzling fans worldwide with spectacular aerial tricks—from the barhop (both legs lifted over the handlebars) to the can-can (one foot is kicked off the pedal and over the handlebars, then returned to the pedal before landing), to the Superman (gripping just the handlebars with the body extended outward, as if flying). Mat's legend grew as he invented more and more tricks.

However, the companies that made the bikes and sponsored teams and events were crashing. There were still a hardcore group of teenagers and younger kids who loved freestyle BMX, but they simply weren't buying enough bikes. Companies began to close.

X Games regular Koji Craft demonstrates the "Superman," one of the stunts that helped freestyle BMX leap in popularity.

Mat left Haro and formed his own Sprocket Jockeys stunt team, enlisting pioneers such as Jay Miron and Dave Mirra. They built a **portable** halfpipe ramp, bought a truck to haul the ramp, and toured

Hiroya Morizaki demonstrates a bike stunt event called flatland, in which rider and bikes work together like dance partners.

the country. They put on shows at bike shops, state fairs, and other places. This was the beginning of Hoffman Promotions, which still organizes shows.

In 1991, Mat started Hoffman Bikes. "I started my bike company because the bikes were not being designed properly for the [growth] of the sport. I was ending up in the hospital because of it," he said in a 2005 online interview. "That inspired me to make a bike that I could trust with my life."

Hoffman bikes continues to sell thousands of extra-sturdy, premium-quality BMX bikes, frames, parts, and clothing every year.

From there, Mat started to organize competitions. He came up with the BS (Bicycle Stunts) Series. The contests weren't just for vert riders, but trail, street, and park riders, too. And rather than traditional win-or-lose competitions, he said the purpose "was to gather with my friends and celebrate who we were and what we did."

As Mat's success—both as a rider and a businessman—continued to soar, he added yet another twist to the BMX scene. He formed Hoffman Sports Association (HSA) as the official organizer of BMX freestyle events. Meanwhile, the television network ESPN recognized the popularity of BMX and other action sports. In 1995, the network asked Mat to help put together a TV competition called the Extreme Games—now known as the X Games. Today, HSA organizes the freestyle BMX events for the X Games and other events, including Mat Hoffman's Crazy Freakin' Bikers Series. The Series is a competition for both amateur and pro riders.

Look Mom, no hands! Bruce Crisman is one of many young riders who have been sponsored by Mat Hoffman's companies.

Hard at Work

Hoffman Bikes has been in business since 1991. Besides making top-notch BMX bikes and accessories, the company sponsors a world-class team of riders. Among the HB stars:

► **Seth Kimbrough** This amazing street rider is also the lead singer in the metal band Mortal Treason.

► **Ryan Barrett** Also known as Captain Euro, this Pittsburgh native can tear it up on the street, the park, and the dirt.

► **Kevin Robinson** (right) One of the top vert riders in the world, he's known for sticking huge 540s and no-handed flairs.

► **Bruce Crisman** When this X Games champ isn't flying off vert ramps, he's grinding on his skateboard or touring with his band, Decoro.

► **Baz Keep** This Englishman is one of the most talented riders to come from the United Kingdom.

CHAPTER 4

It's All About the Adventure

FROM THE BEGINNING, MAT WAS ALL ABOUT getting air on his bike, He could never seem to get enough air, but he kept trying. That's why he progressed from a quarterpipe to a halfpipe. Each time he pedaled back-and-forth along the U-shaped ramp, he'd make higher and higher jumps.

Mat figured out that by building taller ramps, he'd get more and more air. In 1994, he set a world record by flying 23 feet (6 m) off the top of a 21-foot-tall (5.8 m) quarterpipe. Not surprisingly, he wasn't satisfied. So in 2001, he built a taller quarterpipe, with a 400-foot (121-m) runway. He had his partner, Steve Swope, tow him on a motorcycle, reaching speeds of 50 miles (80 km) per hour on the runway. Mat whipped up the ramp and cleared

26.5 feet (8 m) off the top. "I was just over 50 feet off the ground," he said afterward.

In search of even greater heights, Mat combined biking with B.A.S.E. jumping. B.A.S.E. jumpers leap off tall Buildings, Antennas, Spans (bridge, arch or dome)

The little boy who wantd to fly had his dreams come true, but he did it on a bike and not in a plane.

and Earth (cliff or other natural formation) with just a parachute. In June 1997, Mat traveled to Norway to fly off a 3,200-foot (975-m) cliff . . . on a bike!

"I rolled down the rocks, and shot off the edge like a bottle rocket," Mat writes in *The Ride of My Life*. He hurtled toward the ground at 150 miles (241 km) per hour. During a flip, his pant leg got caught in the chain. He managed to free himself, toss the bike, open the chute, and land safely.

Mat Gets Slimed

In one of his more outrageous high-flying stunts, Mat teamed up with Nickelodeon to promote the cable-TV network's 2004 Kids' Choice Awards. He agreed to jump out of an airplane on his BMX bike, from 14,000 feet (4,267 m) above the Arizona desert, and into a pond filled with green slime!

Mat caught some big air from the plane and performed lots of flips before ditching the cycle, pulling the parachute open, and landing safely in the slime.

And what did it feel like to land in a slimy swamp?

"It was weird," he wrote. "That was the hardest part of the whole stunt."

This B.A.S.E. jumper went without a bike, but Mat did a similar jump while riding a bike! He wore a parachute, too, of course!

"I had never felt more alive," Mat said afterward.

Meanwhile, Mat kept winning freestyle BMX events. On his way to 10 world championships, he and other outrageous freestylers raised the sport to new levels of popularity. Mat has introduced stunt riding to million of kids through TV programs, live shows at Universal Studios in Orlando, Florida, appearances in movies, and his Pro BMX video games. He has also teamed up with legendary skateboarder Tony Hawk to perform on Tony's Boom Boom Huck Jam tours of large stadiums and arenas.

Mat was honored at the 2002 EXPN Action Sports and Music Awards with a Lifetime Achievement Award. "I feel like I'm just getting started," he said. To prove it, a few months later at the 2002 X Games, he temporarily came out of retirement. He won a silver medal by completing the first-ever no-handed 900. "We've all thought [about doing this trick], we've all imagined it," said Dave Mirra, the gold medalist. "But imagining it, and doing it, is a whole different world."

That perfectly sums up what Mat Hoffman, now a married man with two young kids, is all about: doing what others can only imagine.

At a video game award ceremony, a trio of action stars showed up: Mat Hoffman, Tony Hawk, and Bam Margera.

Mat Hoffman's Career Highlights

First rider to successfully complete the daring 900, rotating the bike two-and-one-half times in the air off a ramp.

Started Hoffman Bikes with a loan from the Small Business Administration.

Helped ESPN2 produce the early X Games.

Ten-time World Champion BMX biker.

Holds the world record for biggest air by blasting 26.5 feet (8 m) off the vertical halfpipe ramp.

GLOSSARY

amateur   a person who is not paid to perform a certain skill, in this case freestyle BMX

concussion   a brain injury that can range from mild to very serious, usually caused by a blow to the head

elite   the best

portable   able to be carried from place to place with little trouble

revolutions   complete spins around a central point, as when a ball spins on the ground

uncharted   new, unexplored, not yet visited

BOOKS

Ride of His Life: BMX-bike superstar Mat Hoffman uses physics to break world records
By Britt Norlander
(Scholastic, New York) 2004
Science World, September 6, 2004 issue
Volume 61, Issue 1
This magazine article explores how science and daredevilry combine to push Hoffman to new and exciting heights.

The Ride of My Life
By Mat Hoffman
(Regan Books, New York) 2002
This autobiography is stuffed with black-and-white photos of Hoffman performing his most famous stunts.

WEB SITES

Visit our home page for lots of links about Mat Hoffman and freestyle BMX: www.childsworld.com/links

Note to Parents, Teachers, and Librarians: We routinely check our Web links to make sure they're safe, active sites—so encourage your readers to check them out!

INDEX

ABOUT THE AUTHOR

Bob Woods writes and rides motorcycles in Connecticut. He's never done flips like Mat Hoffman, but has ridden his motorcycle all over the United States. Bob has written dozens of books and articles about sports for young readers, covering baseball, basketball, football, and several action sports.